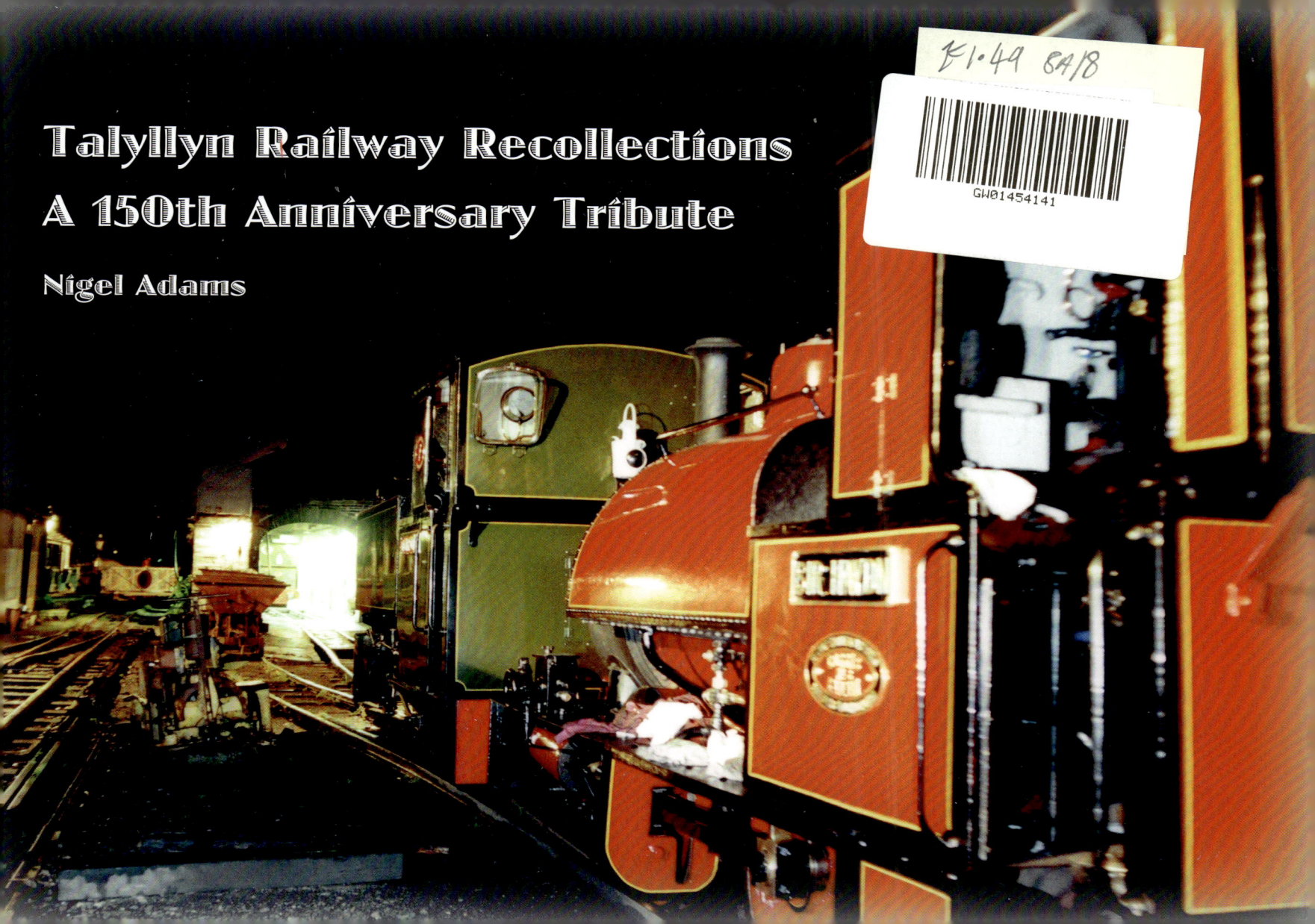

Talyllyn Railway Recollections
A 150th Anniversary Tribute

Nigel Adams

Contents

Acknowledgements

I could not have produced this book without the photographs! The majority have been provided by Ray Reid and David Mitchell, a few are mine and the rest are from a collection the TR possesses, which have been generously given for general publicity use. As it is impossible to credit some of the photographs, I have not individually credited any of them. I hope therefore that all the photographers will accept this general 'thank you', and my personal, very grateful thanks.

I owe a big 'thank you' to Lel Johnson, who did all the typing for me. Typing is not my favourite occupation, and that is putting it mildly! Without Lel's willing help, this book would have taken a lot longer to produce.

Thanks too to David Jones for helping me identify some people in the photographs, and to Lawrie Bowles for proofreading, although it goes without saying that any errors are my responsibility! Finally, without the volunteers, who willingly give their time and skills, the Talyllyn Railway – and many other preserved railways – would not run at all. We have a small paid staff, but they would be the first to admit that it would be impossible to run the railway without the volunteers.

I have been volunteering for more than 30 years and my only regret is that I didn't start earlier! Some of my colleagues have been volunteering for much longer than me and they would not have done that unless it had been enjoyable. As a 'senior citizen' it is very rewarding to see volunteers who started volunteering when teenagers and are now fully qualified guards, blockmen and controllers, and I am sure the same applies to the older loco volunteers.

First published in 2015

British Library Cataloguing in Publication Data

A catalogue record for this book is available from the British Library.

ISBN 978 1 85794 448 8

Silver Link Publishing Ltd
The Trundle
Ringstead Road
Great Addington
Kettering
Northants NN14 4BW

Tel/Fax: 01536 330588
email: sales@nostalgiacollection.com
Website: www.nostalgiacollection.com

Printed and bound in the Czech Republic

Title page: Loco Nos 7 and 3, *Tom Rolt* and *Sir Haydn*, in Pendre yard at night.

Introduction

Wharf Station Tywyn

This book is the second entitled *Talyllyn Railway Recollections* in this 'Nostalgia Collection' series. The first, published in 2010, marked the 60th anniversary of the Talyllyn Railway Preservation Society (TRPS), founded in October 1950. The first train to run under the auspices of the TRPS ran from Wharf station to Rhydyronen station on 14 May 1951, which is marked each year as 'Founder's Day'.

This book is published to mark the 150th anniversary of the Talyllyn Railway Company, which legally came into existence on 5 July 1865. It was originally built to carry slate from Bryn Eglwys Quarry in the hills above Abergynolwyn to the coast at Tywyn, to be delivered to places all over the world.

The story of the railway has been told in a number of books, which are on sale in the Railway Shop and are well worth a read. But one vitally important fact should not be forgotten: without volunteers the Talyllyn Railway could not operate. We currently have a dedicated band – both young and old – but we need a steady supply of new volunteers to ensure the future operation of the world's first preserved steam railway.

Any volunteer will tell you that it is very rewarding and you meet new friends. Why not give it a try?

TYWYN A train approaches the British Railways signal box at Tywyn (long since gone), as seen from a southbound train.

Above: **TYWYN's** BR station can be glimpsed beyond the signal box in this view taken from the road bridge in Neptune Road. Many photographs of main-line and Talyllyn Railway trains have been taken from this bridge.

Right: **TYWYN** Loco No 2 *Dolgoch* heads a train at the Talyllyn Railway's Wharf station before it was rebuilt.

Above: **TYWYN** A sad occasion: the body of Graham Jenkins, a Talyllyn Railway employee who died at the tragically early age of 33, is taken from the hearse to board the train to take him on his last trip on the railway.

TYWYN No 2 *Dolgoch* is being unloaded from a 'Weltrol' wagon on the main-line siding after having been away from Tywyn.

Right: **TYWYN** Nos 1 *Talyllyn* and 2 *Dolgoch* stand on the middle road at Wharf with the 'Museum Slate Train', i.e. the slate wagons, a covered van and Van 6.

Left: **TYWYN** No 7 *Tom Rolt* heads a mixed train in the middle road prior to the rebuilding of Wharf station in 2004/05.

Below right: **TYWYN** The slate wagons are seen again on the middle road of the modern Wharf station, with an incline wagon and a van. The van had been used as a store, located on the bank on the left-hand side just on the Nant Gwernol side of Rhydyronen bridge.

Above left: **TYWYN** No 2 *Dolgoch* (cab-less), some slate wagons and one of the original Talyllyn Railway coaches stand in Wharf station yard.

Above: **TYWYN** The first stage of the Wharf station redevelopment is under way. This was done first because the much bigger second stage had not been finalised, but funds were unexpectedly available to cover the first stage.

Left: **TYWYN** No 6 *Douglas* brings a train into Wharf station, unusually facing west rather than towards Nant Gwernol.

Above: **TYWYN**
No 7 *Tom Rolt* stands
in the yard at Wharf
waiting to take over
its train.

Right: **TYWYN**
Loco No 6 is turned
using the crane on
the lorry that had just
delivered No 10 in
1997. David Jones and
Chris Price look on.

Left: **PENDRE** A view of Pendre from School Bridge, looking north-east up the line towards Nant Gwernol.

Above and right: **PENDRE** Before the present block post (signal box) was built at Pendre, there were lever frames at each end of the loop and the blockman had to walk between the two frames to cross trains. The first photograph shows the frame at the west end of the loop, and the second the frame at the east end. The driver in the second photograph is the late Ray Smith.

Left: **PENDRE** This photograph shows the interior of Pendre block post as it is today – much easier to operate, and the blockman is protected from the elements!

Below left: **PENDRE** The Pendre blockman (your author) has let an up train into the loop, reset the road for a down train and put the Wharf-Pendre token through the token machine; he is now giving the down train the flag as it approaches Pendre level crossing gates.

Below: **PENDRE** The tokens are now exchanged with the driver of the down train, and the surrendered Brynglas-Pendre token will be put through the token machine, the road reset and the up train driver given the token to allow his train to depart.

Right: **PENDRE**
The second stage of the building of the West Carriage Shed at Pendre, behind the block post.

Below: **PENDRE**
Driver Viv Thorpe on loco No 3 *Sir Haydn* brings his up train through Pendre yard, past the North Carriage Shed on the right, during the AGM day in 1989.

Above: **PENDRE** Loco No 2 *Dolgoch* reverses up the main line at Pendre past the block post. When it gets beyond the furthest points, they will be set for the West Carriage Shed (on the left of the picture), and No 2 will enter to couple up to the empty stock of its train.

PENDRE No 1 *Talyllyn* draws empty stock out of the North Carriage Shed; the original TR brake van (Van 5) is next to the loco.

Main picture: **PENDRE**
Pendre yard at night, with the shed and Works on the right.

Inset right: **PENDRE**
All the TR's steam locos line up in Pendre yard in reverse numerical order from the front, i.e. Nos 7, 6, 4, 3, 2 and 1, while three loco volunteers stand next to the main line. This was on the occasion of 1999 TRPS Annual General Meeting. The middle volunteer is the late Tony Bennett.

Inset far right: **PENDRE**
Loco No 3 *Sir Haydn* – in Corris Railway livery – poses in Pendre yard.

Left: **PENDRE** No 2 *Dolgoch* runs round to its empty stock in Pendre yard, possibly so it can propel it to Wharf station.

Top right: **PENDRE** No 1 *Talyllyn* is prepared for a day's work in the loco shed.

Bottom right: **PENDRE** No 2 *Dolgoch* is coaled up at Pendre, viewed from inside the shed. It is thought that the driver is Herbert Jones and the fireman Brian Green.

Far right: **PENDRE** Loco No 3 *Sir Haydn* in bits in Pendre Works. The late John Slater is working on the milling machine.

Below: **PENDRE** The Stanton coach nears completion outside the West Carriage Shed at Pendre, with Don Newing on the roof.

PENDRE WORKS Two fine examples of the high quality of work carried out at Pendre Works are seen here. A Glyn Valley Tramway 1st Class coach stands at Wharf station with its door open and the red carpet down ready to receive a VIP passenger, and Van 5 is seen at Abergynolwyn station.

Above: **PENDRE WORKS** opposite the station platform, is seen just after the flower-bed, the plants and the stones have been made nice and tidy.

Above right: **PENDRE** A Talyllyn Railway coach receives attention in the Paint Shop at Pendre.

Right: **PENDRE** The boiler of loco No 4 *Edward Thomas* is worked on in Pendre Works.

Above: **PENDRE** At the north-east end of the layout is Pendre platform; the table and benches are occupied for the works tea-break when the weather is suitable!

Left and above:
PENDRE The inaugural train for the opening of the Nant Gwernol extension in 1976 stands in Pendre yard. The driver is the late Dai Jones and the fireman the late Phil Guest. Standing between them is the late Herbert Jones.

Right: **PENDRE**
Two trains crossing at Pendre.

Above: **PENDRE** Unloading wagons at Pendre platform.

Above: **PENDRE** Loco No 4 *Edward Thomas* passes over Pendre level crossing with a down train before the new gates were installed.

Above: **RHYDYRONEN** Driver Mike Green brings his train into Rhydyronen. The loco is No 4 *Edward Thomas.*

Below: **RHYDYRONEN** Driver John Hague brings a special train into the station headed by loco No 7 *Tom Rolt*.

Above: **RHYDYRONEN** No 2 *Dolgoch* pauses at Rhydyronen with an up train. Martin Lester stands by the engine.

Right: **RHYDYRONEN**
Dolgoch is seen again leaving Rhydyronen with a down train. Note the rail lengths stored at the end of the platform, which indicates that some relaying work had recently been done.

Brynglas

BRYNGLAS A superb shot of a mixed train standing on the main line at Brynglas. This was almost certainly a special train for photographers.

Inset: **BRYNGLAS** A crossing at Brynglas. The up train (right) stands on the main line while the down train passes through the loop on its way to Wharf station.

Below: **BRYNGLAS** A Driver Experience train headed by loco No 2 *Dolgoch* stands on the main line at Brynglas waiting for a down train to pass through the loop.

Right: **BRYNGLAS** Long-standing volunteer John Smallwood is seen setting the road in Brynglas block post.

Dolgoch

Above: **DOLGOCH** Dolgoch Viaduct towers above the footpath from Dolgoch Falls.

Left: **DOLGOCH** Loco No 1 *Talyllyn* heads a train in Dolgoch Woods.

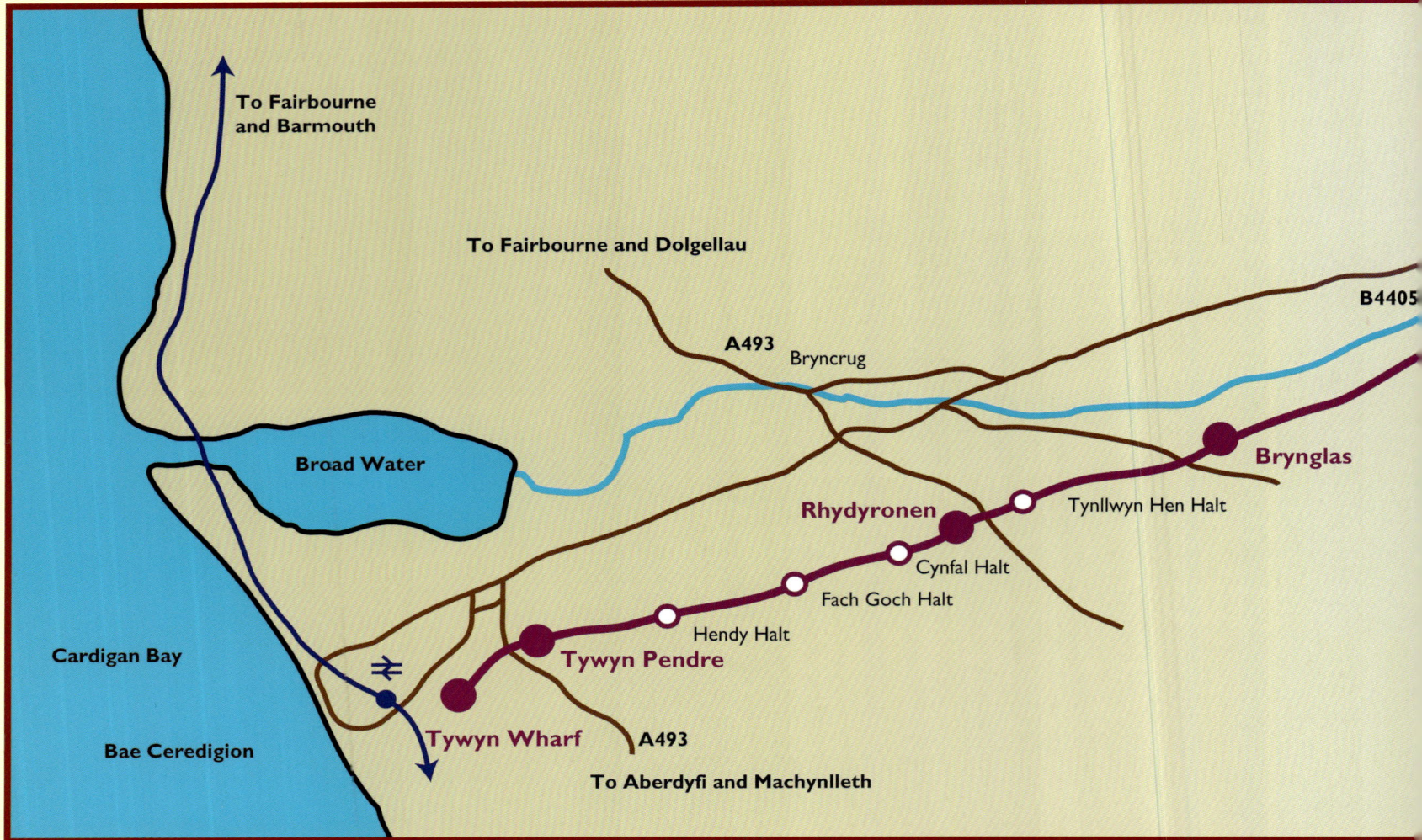

To Fairbourne
and Barmouth

To Fairbourne and Dolgellau

B4405

A493

Bryncrug

Brynglas

Broad Water

Tynllwyn Hen Halt

Rhydyronen

Cynfal Halt

Fach Goch Halt

Hendy Halt

Cardigan Bay

Tywyn Pendre

Bae Ceredigion

Tywyn Wharf

A493

To Aberdyfi and Machynlleth

B4405

Abergynolwyn Village

Abergynolwyn

Quarry Siding Halt

Dolgoch

Nant Gwernol

Site of Bryn Eglwys Slate Quarries

Dolgoch Falls and Ravine

THE TALYLLYN RAILWAY COMPANY

Rheilffordd TALYLLYN Railway ROUTE MAP

Stations Halts

Talyllyn Railway

Main line railway

Main roads

Rivers / streams

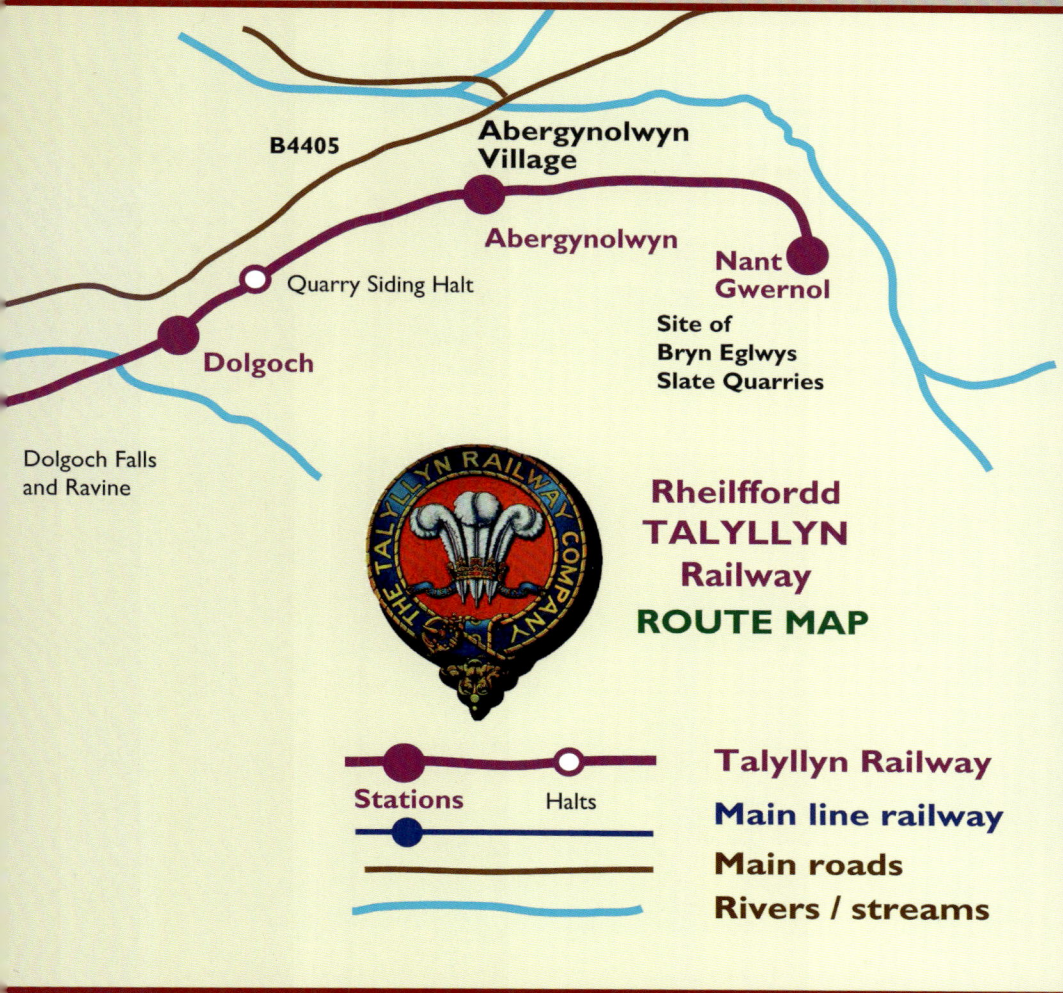

DOLGOCH No 2 brings an up train across Dolgoch Viaduct.

Above: **DOLGOCH** Loco No 6 *Douglas* takes water at Dolgoch station.

Above right: **DOLGOCH** No 3 takes water from the old water tower at Dolgoch. Driver Gareth Jones and Fireman Karen Willans ensure that the chute is in the correct place, while the guard watches from his seat in the sun on the platform.

Right: **DOLGOCH** Having filled the tank with water, the same train sets off from the station. It is a mixed train, which means it is probably a photographic special.

Below: **DOLGOCH** The Driver Experience train seen earlier at Brynglas takes on water at Dolgoch station.

Above: **DOLGOCH** No 6 *Douglas* waits at Dolgoch with a down train.

Above: **QUARRY SIDING** Driver Graham Thomas brings the Vintage Train into Quarry Siding with loco No 1 *Talyllyn*.

Right: **QUARRY SIDING** Three trains at Quarry Siding all at once!

WHISTLE

Above: **QUARRY SIDING** *Talyllyn* is seen again, standing at the down stop board at Quarry Siding, waiting for the flag signal from the blockman. The driver is the late Dai Jones.

Right: **QUARRY SIDING** Having set the road and given the flag to *Talyllyn*, the blockman exchanges tokens with the fireman while the up train stands on the main line. There is now a white sighting board in front of the block post door against which the blockman waves the flag, to improve visibility for loco crews of down trains.

ABERGYNOLWYN

No 1 *Talyllyn* brings a special train up the loop into Abergynolwyn station. The train arrives at the platform and the passengers alight.

It is being driven by fireman James Foster, while the driver, Bill Heynes, takes a turn at firing and keeping a look out.

Above: **ABERGYNOLWYN**
The block post diagram in Abergynolwyn box.

Above: **ABERGYNOLWYN**
Another up train arrives at Abergynolwyn headed by *Talyllyn*, but this time it is photographed further up the platform.

Right: **ABERGYNOLWYN**
The blockman, David Benjamin takes the Quarry Siding-Abergynolwyn token from the fireman of an up train and gives him the staff and tickets for the journey from here to Nant Gwernol and back.

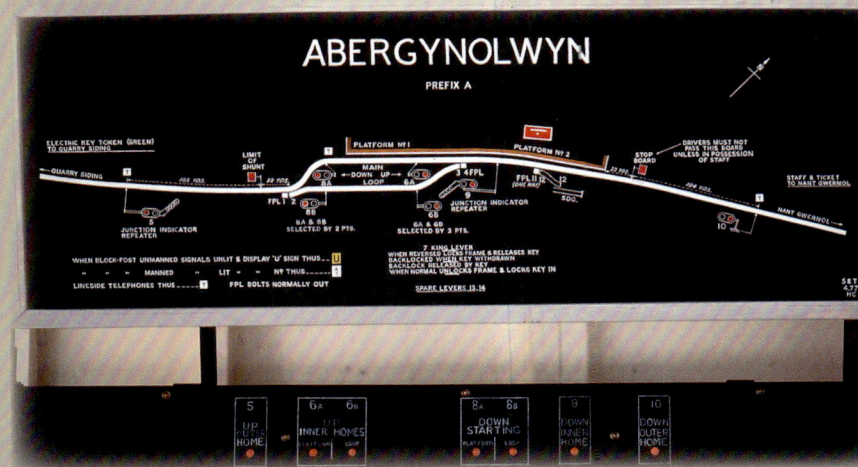

Right: **ABERGYNOLWYN**
Trains cross at Abergynolwyn in about 1976 or 1977, with the down train standing in the west platform.

Above: **ABERGYNOLWYN** The down train on the first day of operation in 2007 leaves Abergynolwyn wreathed in steam. It must have been cold that day as the guard (your author) is wearing his BR greatcoat!

Above: **NANT GWERNOL** An up train has just arrived at Nant Gwernol and the locomotive, No 1 *Talyllyn*, has uncoupled to run round ready to depart on the down journey.

Talyllyn people

Right: **ABERGYNOLWYN**
The Talyllyn Railway is always welcoming to visitors, and one way of encouraging the volunteers of the future is to let them have their photograph taken by or on an engine, waving a flag or in a signal box. Here is the author's younger grandson standing on the running board of loco No 5 *Midlander* with driver Chris Johnson alongside, during a Family Fun Day at Abergynolwyn.

Above: **WHARF** Loco No 2 *Dolgoch*, during a test run between Pendre and Wharf station, stands at the platform at Wharf while David Black makes some sort of adjustment; driver David Jones and Nick Fieldhouse wait on the footplate. John Robinson looks on.

Right: The Jones family have been involved with the TR for three generations. Here is Hugh (known as 'Father') on the footplate of No 6 *Douglas*. He lived in a cottage ('Plas Coch') next to the line at Rhydyronen. He had two sons (Herbert and Dai) and David, seen in the previous picture, is Dai's son.

Left:
ABERGYNOLWYN
Here he is again at Abergynolwyn block post with blockman Matthew Wear, and volunteer Marc Smith in the background.

Locomotives and rolling stock

Above: **TYWYN** Mike Green is on the footplate of No 2 *Dolgoch* at Wharf station on the occasion of his last driving turn. Mike was an employee in the Workshop for many years (as well as being a driver), and he continues to volunteer following his retirement.

Left: **TYWYN** No 1 *Talyllyn* returns to terra firma at Wharf station.

Below: **TYWYN** No 2 *Dolgoch* and some wagons stand on the middle road at Wharf.

Left: **TYWYN** No 6 *Douglas* is also seen on the platform road.

Below: **TYWYN and PENDRE** Two further views of *Douglas*, on the coal road at Wharf and standing next to the ash wagon at Pendre shed.

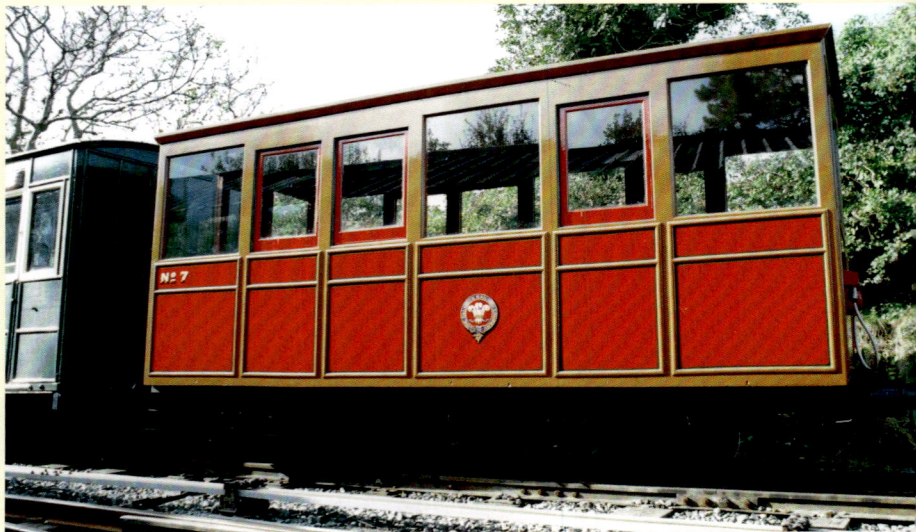

Above and below: **TYWYN** Two photographs of No 8 *Merseysider* at Wharf station, the first showing the Ruston & Hornsby diesel in original 'as delivered' condition, and the second as first modified.

Above: **PENDRE** Van 7, built by Jack McCanna, at Pendre.

Left: **PENDRE** The Corris Railway 'mail-waggon' in Pendre yard.

Right: **BRYNGLAS** Two vintage coaches (left and middle) at Brynglas.

Church connections (Part 2)

In the first *Talyllyn Railway Recollections* volume there was a short section entitled 'Church connections'. Here are some more photographs under that heading.

Left: During an Archdeacon's Visitation for the parishes in South Merioneth, the Venerable Andrew Jones, Archdeacon of Merioneth, stands beside loco No 2 *Dolgoch*, having travelled from Wharf station on the footplate.

Above: On 4 May 2012 the Bishop of Bangor, Andy John, and the Bishop of Sodor & Man, Robert Patterson, shared a Driver Experience train. Here driver Mike Green goes through the Safety Briefing with Bishop Andy in the Loco Office at Pendre.

Above: Bishop Andy and Bishop Robert with the crew: driver Mike Green, fireman Duncan Ritchie and (extreme left) the guard, your author.

Right: The Bishops stand in front of No 2 *Dolgoch* in Pendre yard during the layover there between trips to allow the loco to be coaled and watered.

Left: The Bishops with Mike Green after he had presented them with their certificates. Driver Experience trains on the TR are increasingly popular and participants tell us that they are very good value.

Left: NEAR BRYNGLAS
Loco No 3 *Sir Haydn*, in Corris Railway livery, heads an up train over the farm crossing above Brynglas station.

Right: TALYLLYN LAKE
Not surprisingly, many people think that the Talyllyn Railway runs by Talyllyn Lake, but it doesn't. The lake is about 3 miles further on from Abergynolwyn station, but is well worth a visit by road, as shown by this photograph, taken in February 2012.

Endpiece

PENDRE A train leaves Pendre station, where all journeys start and end because that is where the locos and rolling stock are stored.

Index of locations, locomotives and Talyllyn people